The electromagnetic spectrum

Galileo's x20 telescope

William Herschel's 40-foot reflecting telescope

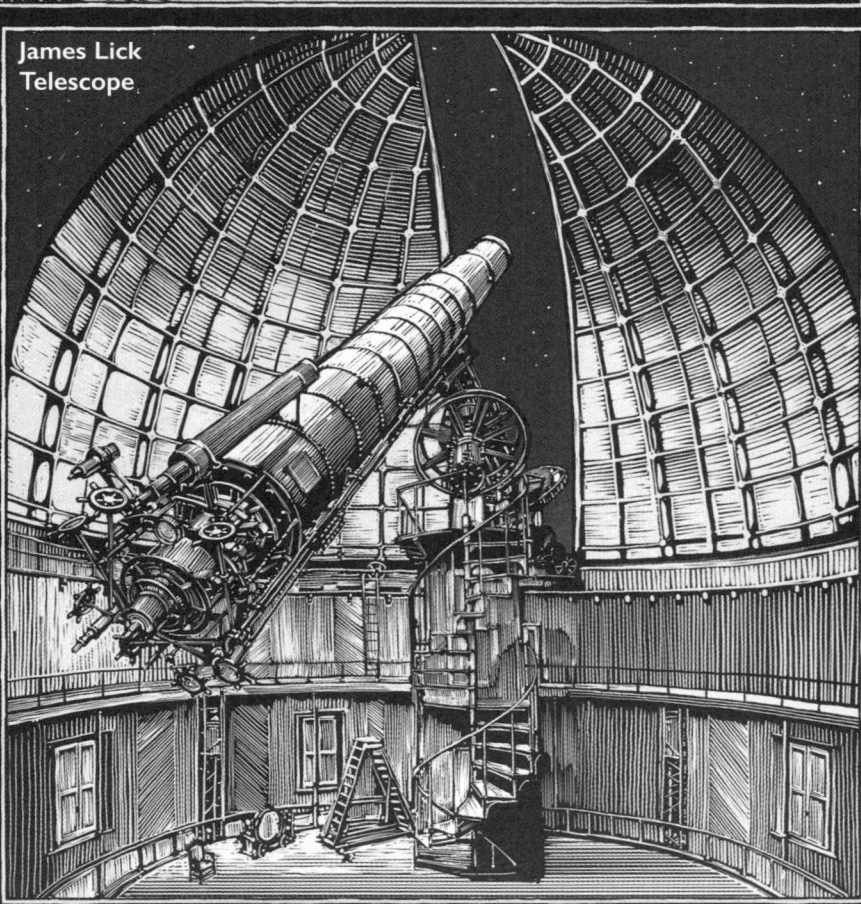

James Lick Telescope

James Lick Telescope

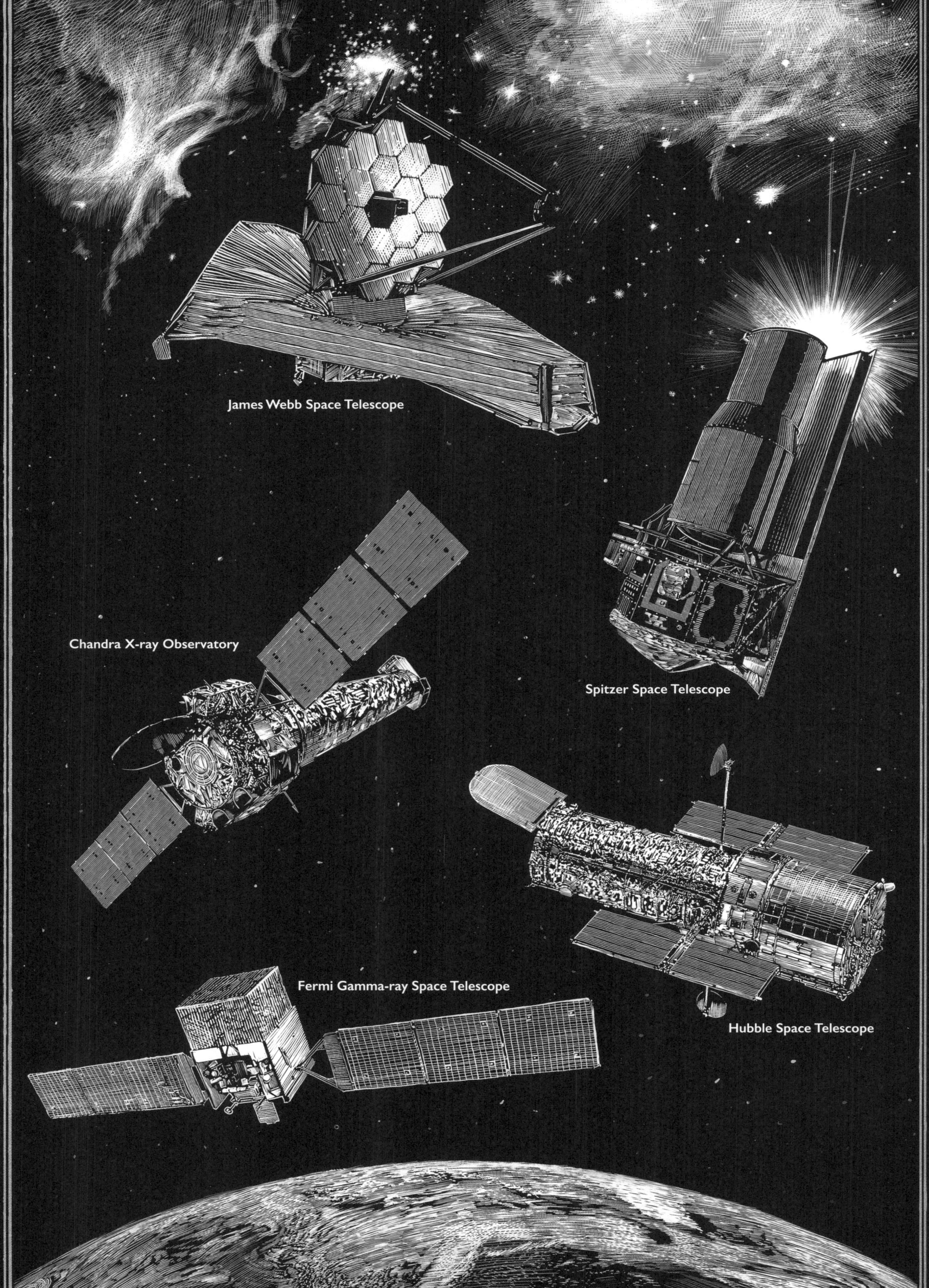

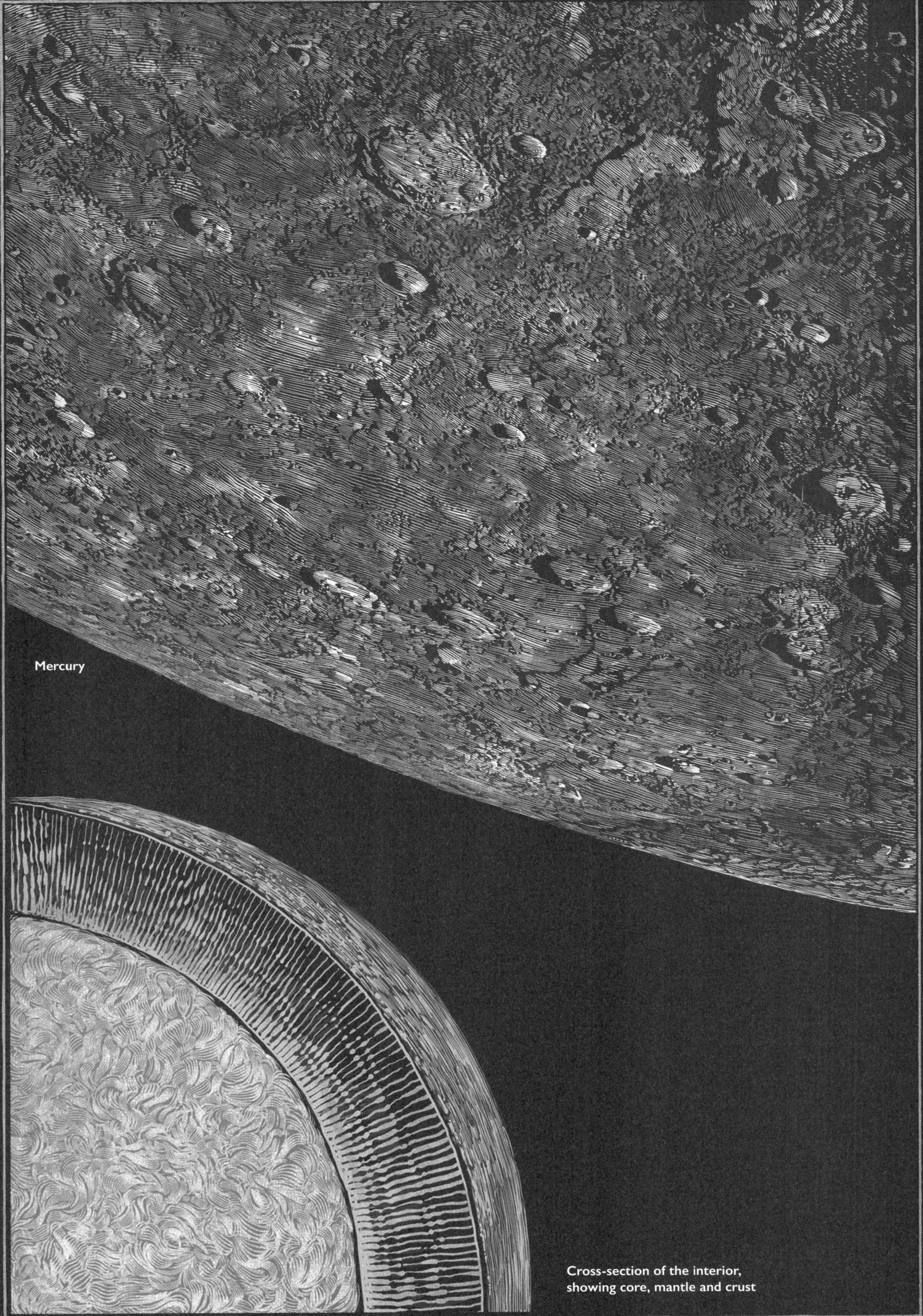

Mercury

Cross-section of the interior, showing core, mantle and crust

Earth

The far side of the Moon

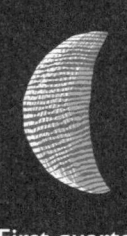
Waxing crescent

First quarter

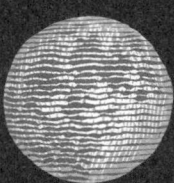
Waxing gibbous

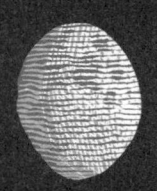
Full moon

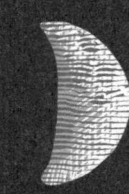
Waning gibbous

Last quarter

Waning crescent

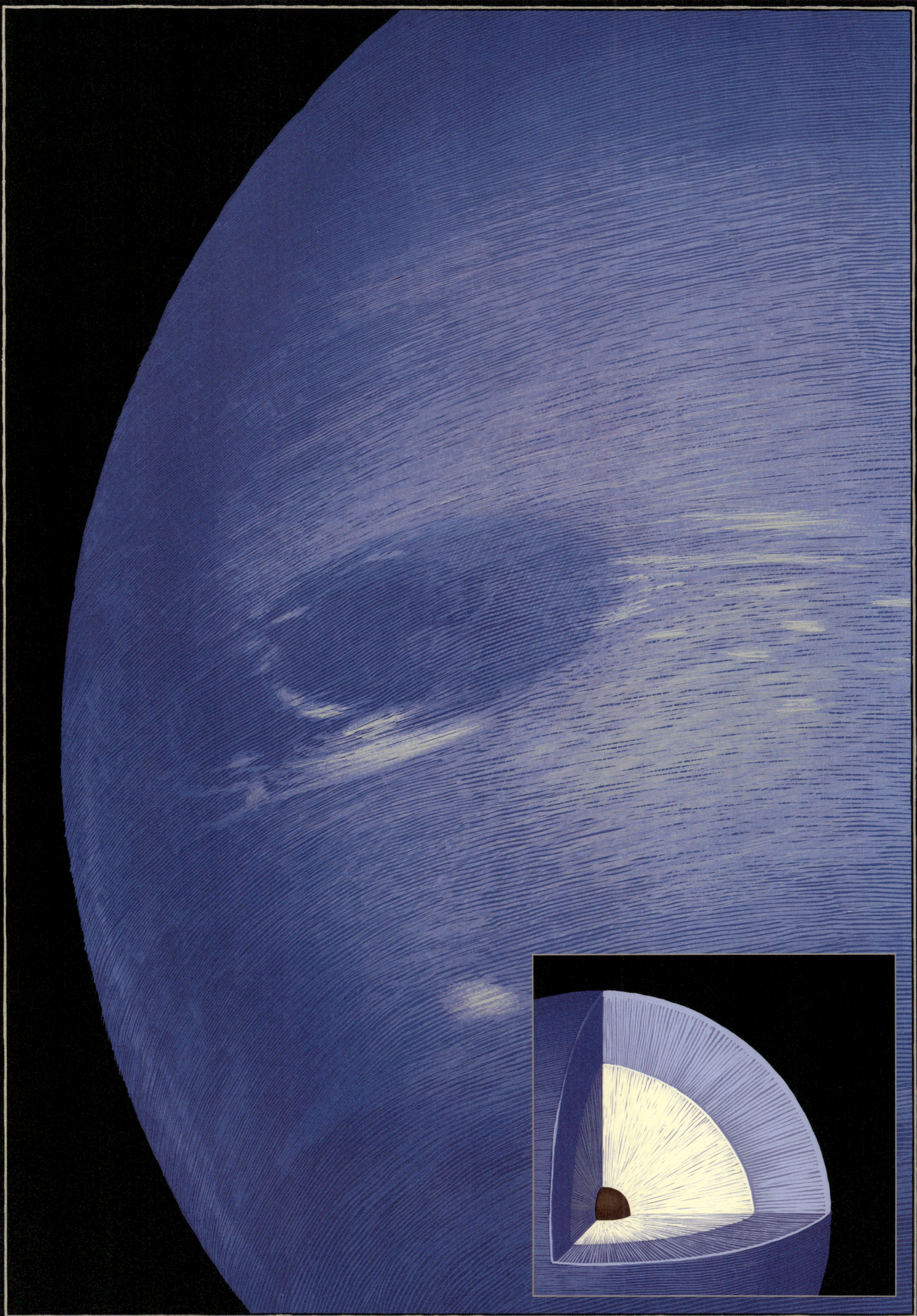

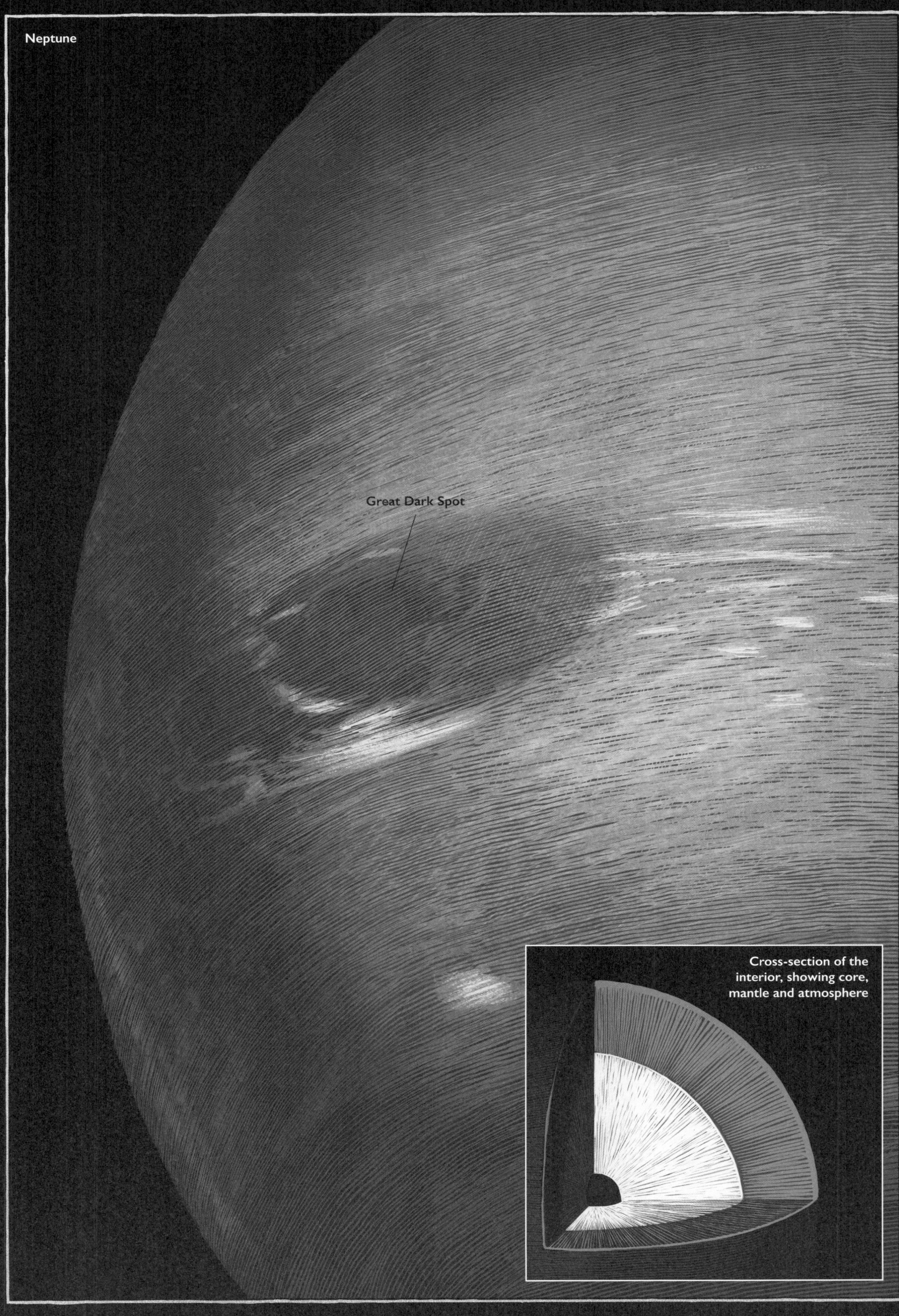

Exoplanet 55 Cancri e (aka Janssen)

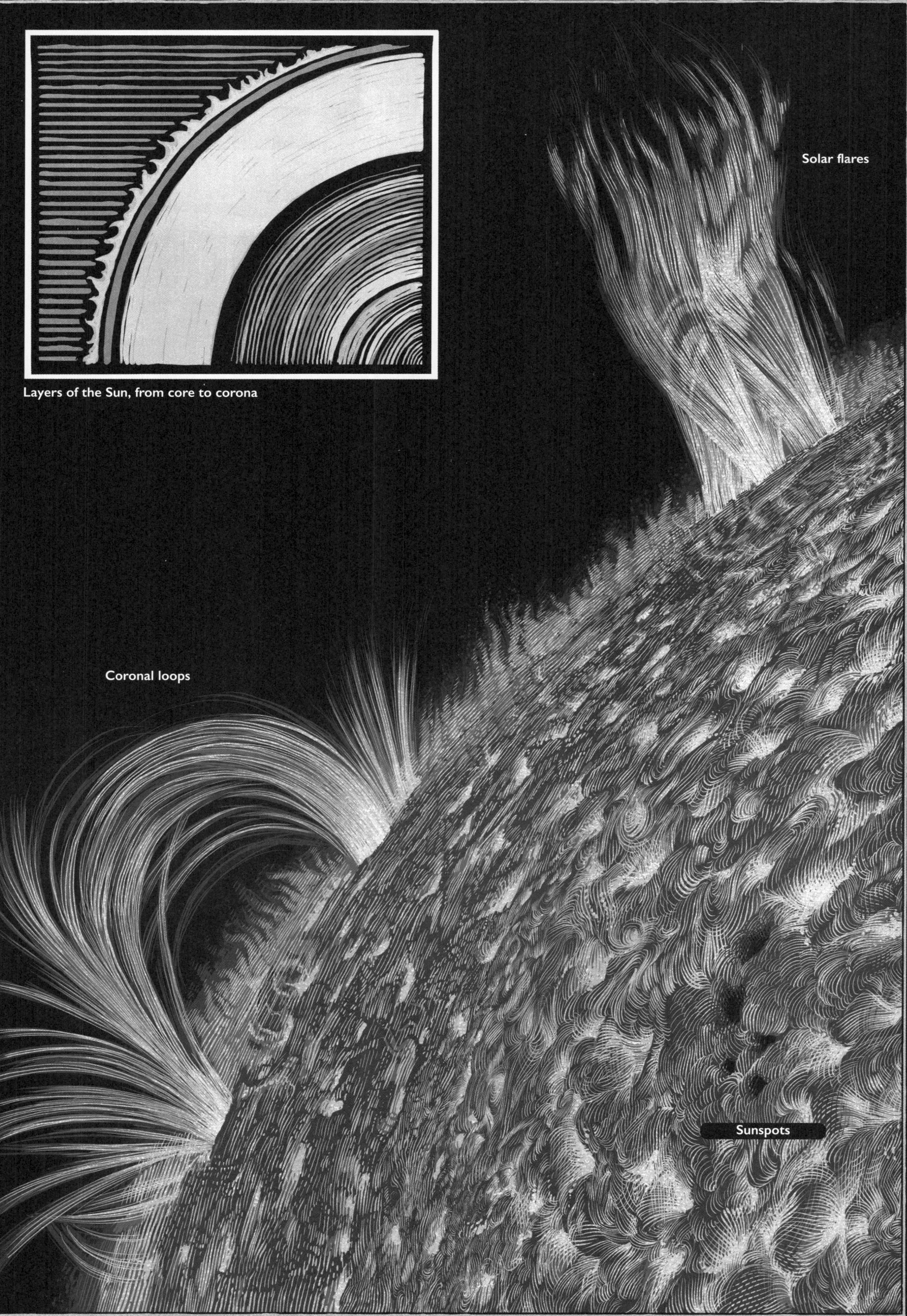

Magnetic fields

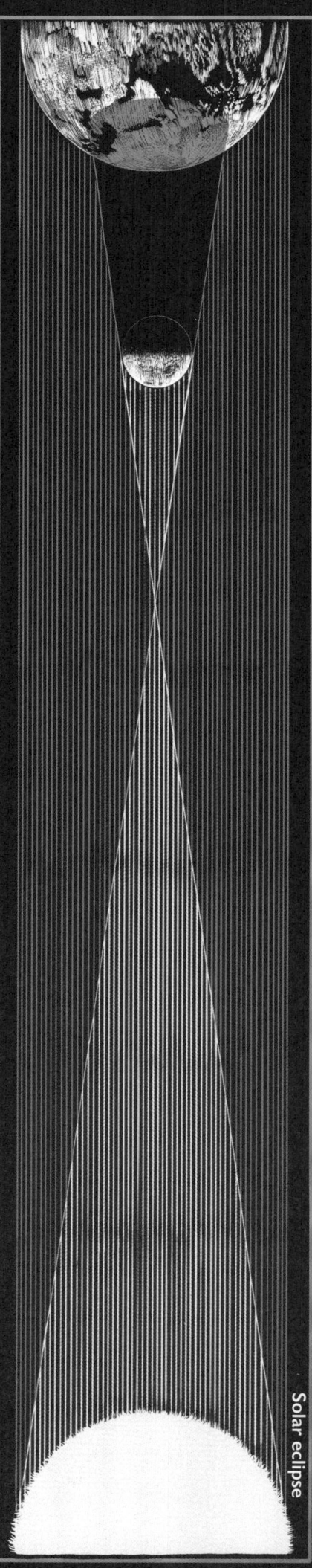

Solar eclipse

The Sun's corona

Northern hemisphere constellations

Southern hemisphere constellations

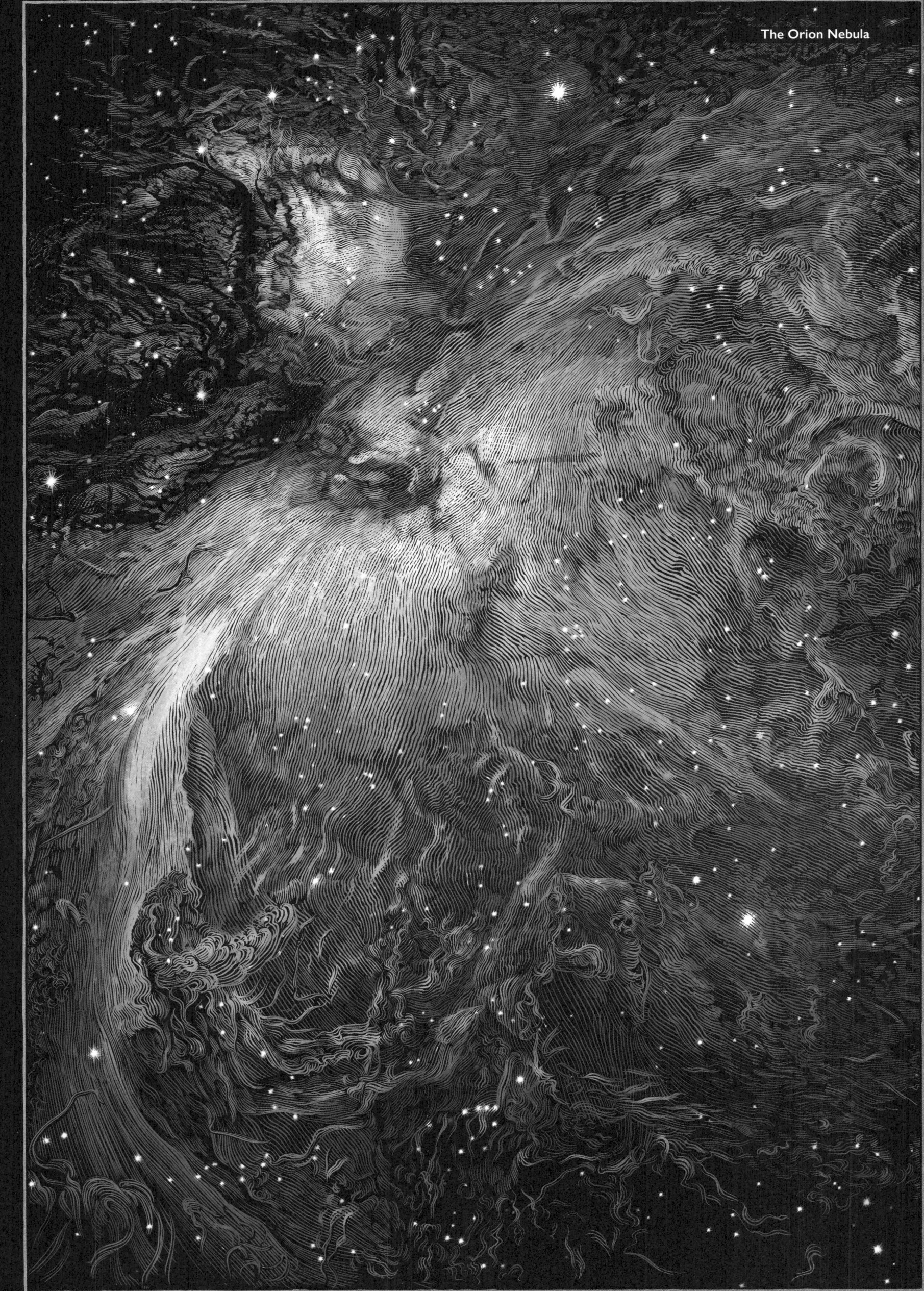

The Orion Nebula

Interstellar nebula

Protostar

Lightweight star life cycle

Middleweight star life cycle

Heavyweight star life cycle

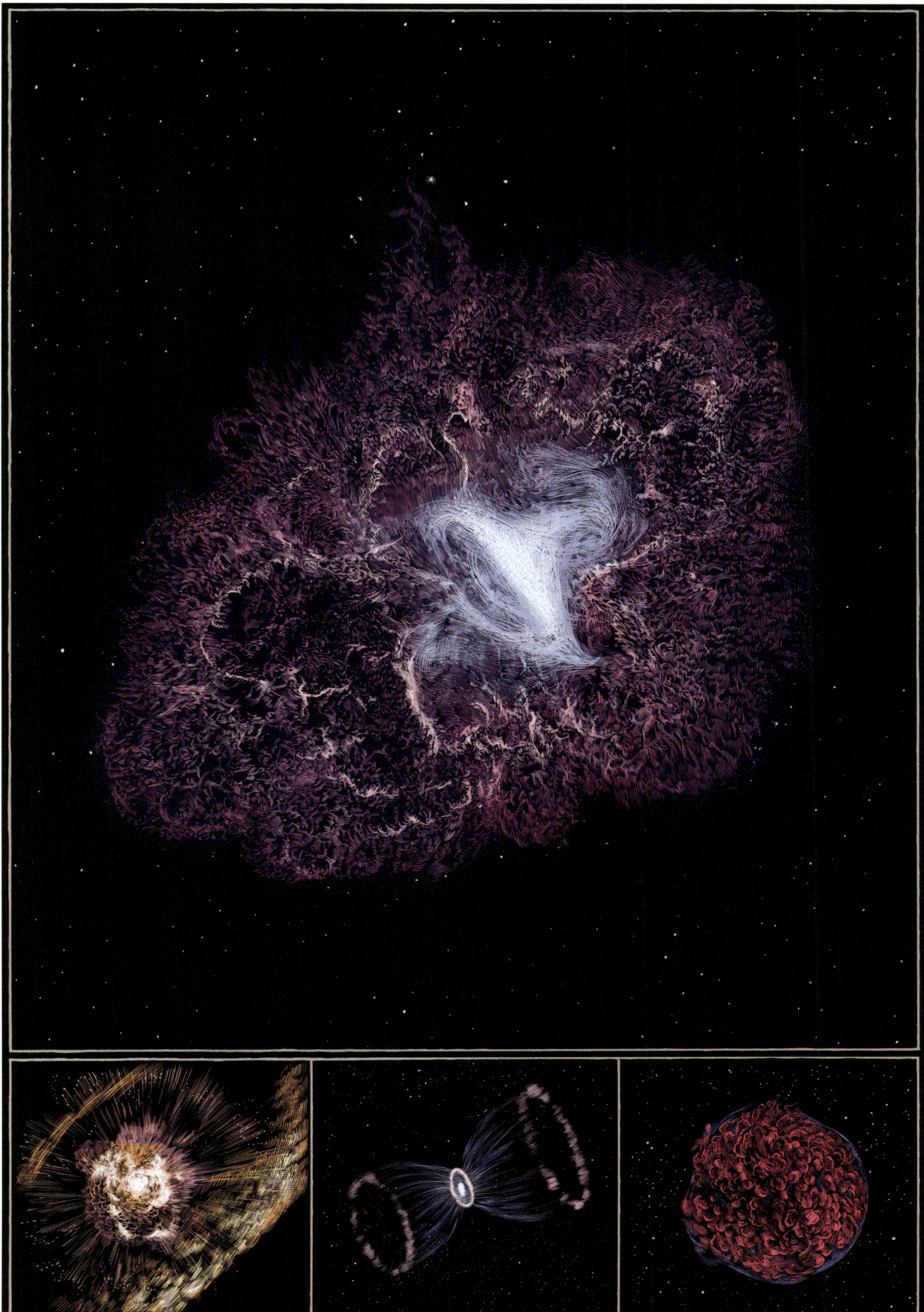

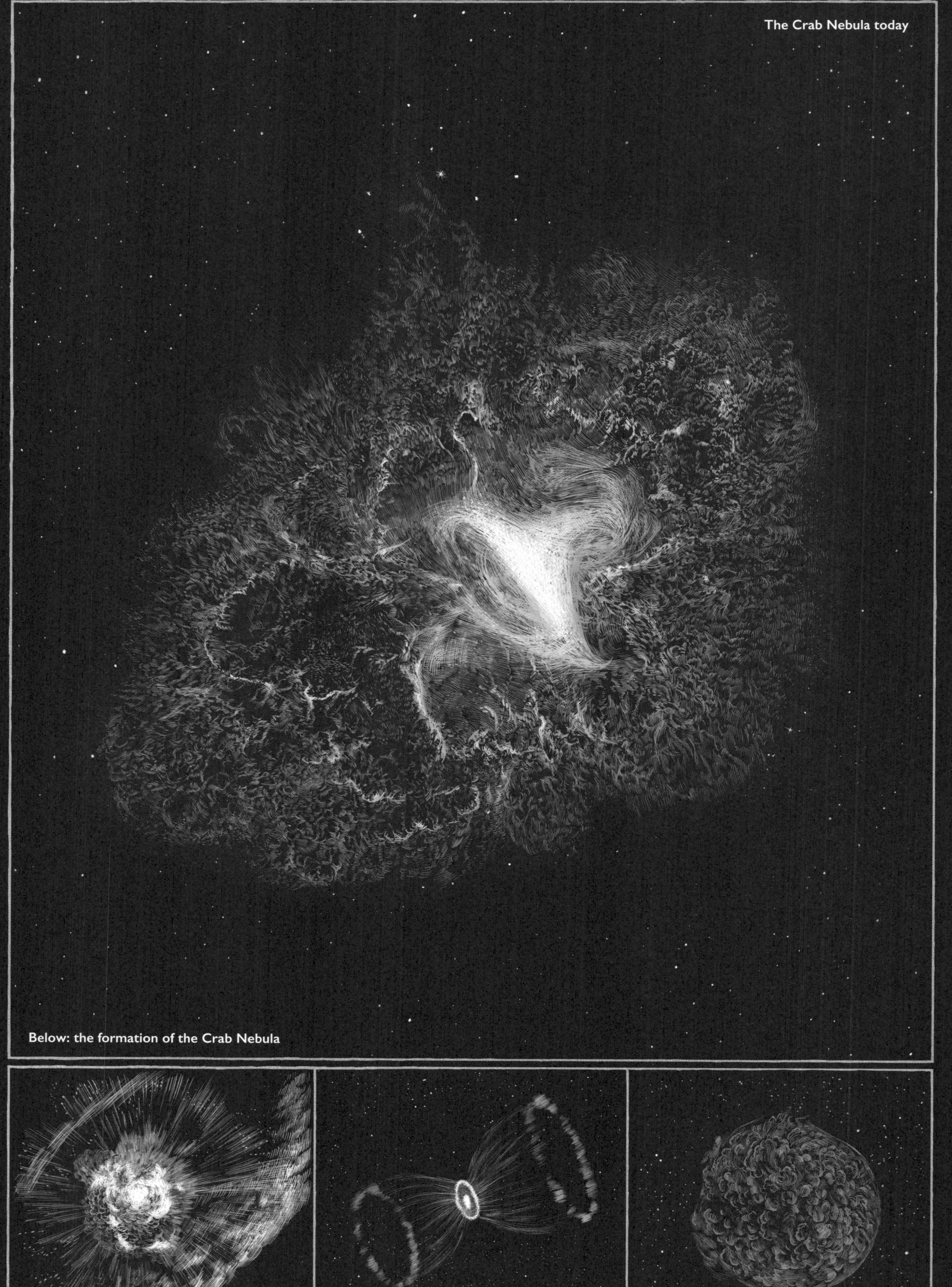

The Crab Nebula today

Below: the formation of the Crab Nebula

Supernova explosion

The aftermath of the explosion

The supernova remnant

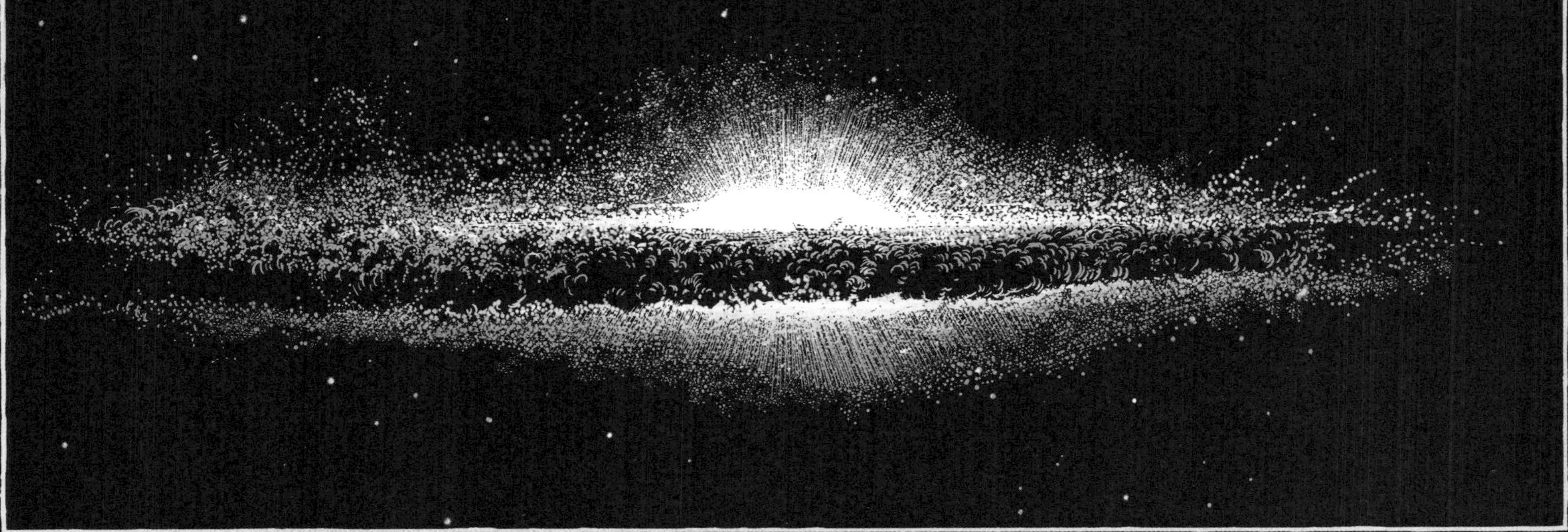

The Milky Way Galaxy
(viewed from the side)

The Milky Way Galaxy
(viewed from above)

Arp 273, a 'rose of galaxies'

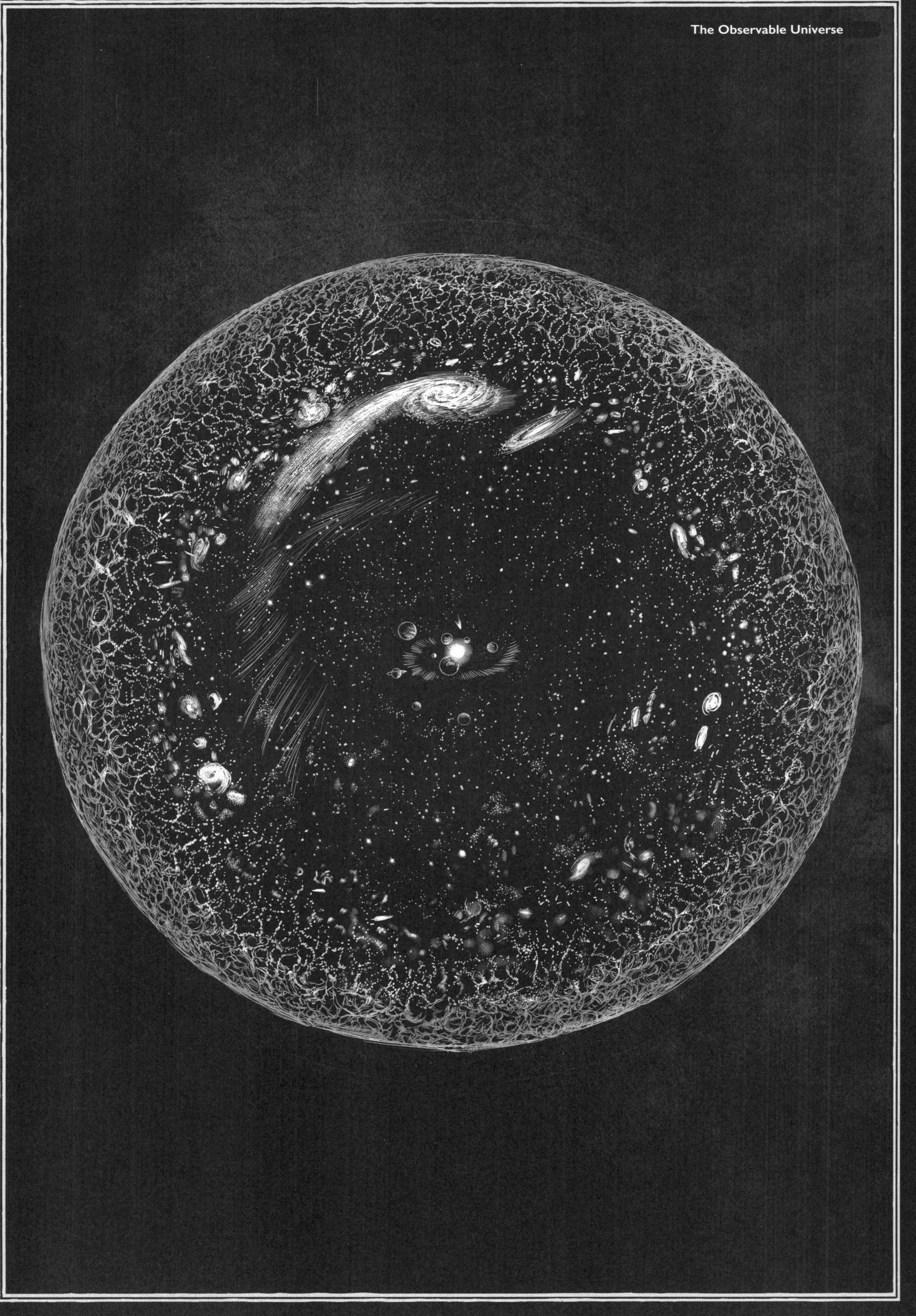

The Observable Universe

The Runaway Universe

The Big Rip

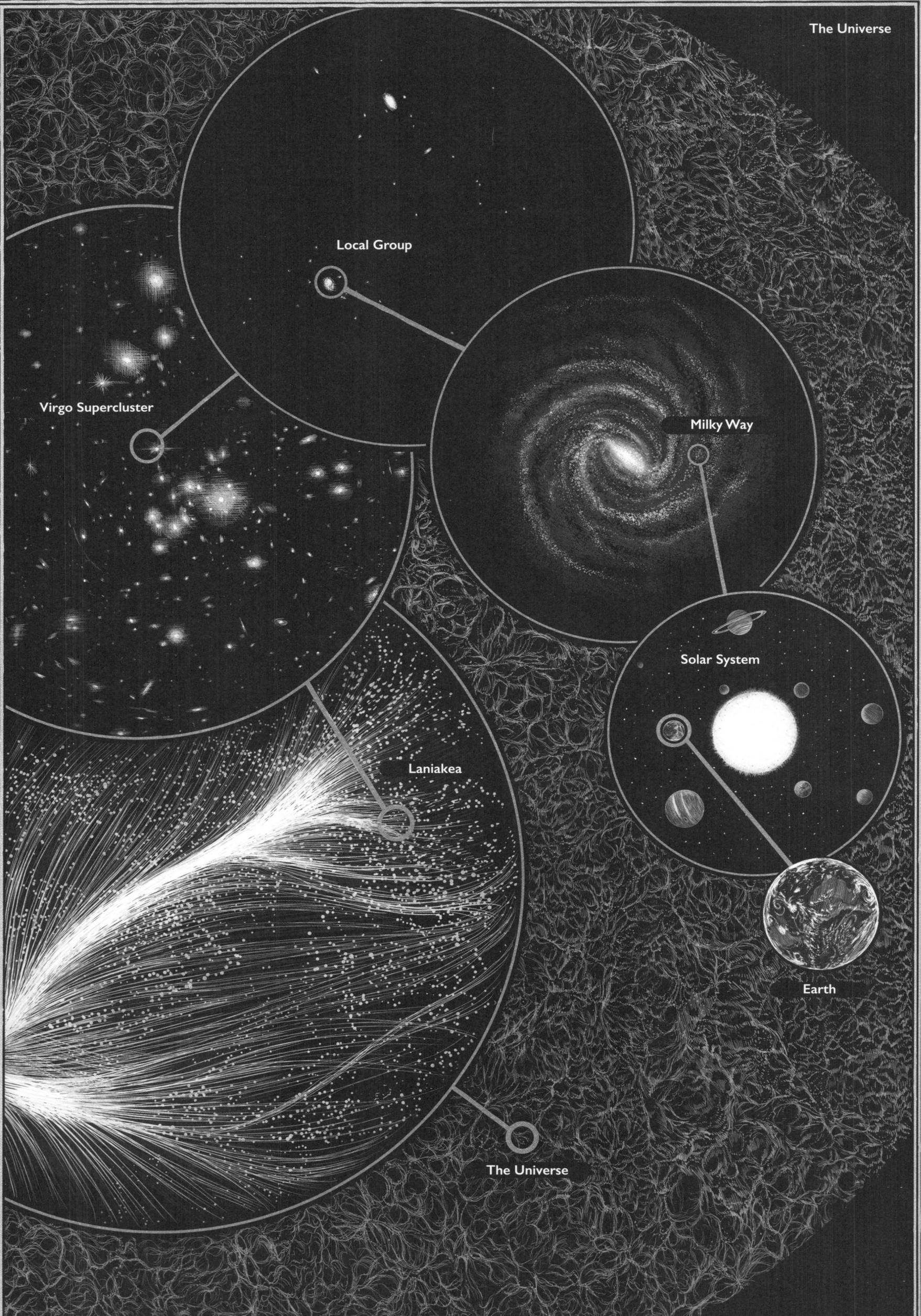